Ferishtah's Fancies by Robert Browning

Robert Browning is one of the most significant Victorian Poets and, of course, English Poetry.

Much of his reputation is based upon his mastery of the dramatic monologue although his talents encompassed verse plays and even a well-regarded essay on Shelley during a long and prolific career.

He was born on May 7th, 1812 in Walmouth, London. Much of his education was home based and Browning was an eclectic and studious student, learning several languages and much else across a myriad of subjects, interests and passions.

Browning's early career began promisingly. The fragment from his intended long poem Pauline brought him to the attention of Dante Gabriel Rossetti, and was followed by Paracelsus, which was praised by both William Wordsworth and Charles Dickens. In 1840 the difficult Sordello, which was seen as willfully obscure, brought his career almost to a standstill.

Despite these artistic and professional difficulties his personal life was about to become immensely fulfilling. He began a relationship with, and then married, the older and better known Elizabeth Barrett. This new foundation served to energise his writings, his life and his career.

During their time in Italy they both wrote much of their best work. With her untimely death in 1861 he returned to London and thereafter began several further major projects.

The collection Dramatis Personae (1864) and the book-length epic poem The Ring and the Book (1868-69) were published and well received; his reputation as a venerated English poet now assured.

Robert Browning died in Venice on December 12th, 1889.

Index of Contents

FERISHTAH'S FANCIES

NOTE

There is a loose connection between this group of poems and certain forms of Oriental literature, notably The Fables of Bidpai or Pilpay, Firdausi's Sháh-Námeh, and the Book of Job; specific instances may easily be noted; but Browning himself said in a letter to a friend, written soon after the publication of Ferishtah's Fancies: "I hope and believe that one or two careful readings of the Poem will make its sense clear enough. Above all, pray allow for the Poet's inventiveness in any case, and do not suppose there is more than a thin disguise of a few Persian names and allusions. There was no such person as Ferishtah—the stories are all inventions.... The Hebrew quotations are put in for a purpose, as a direct acknowledgment that certain doctrines may be found in the Old Book, which the Concoctors of Novel Schemes of Morality put forth as discoveries of their own."

PROLOGUE

Pray, Reader, have you eaten ortolans
Ever in Italy?
Recall how cooks there cook them: for my plan 's
To—Lyre with Spit ally.
They pluck the birds,—some dozen luscious lumps,
Or more or fewer,—
Then roast them, heads by heads and rumps by rumps,
Stuck on a skewer.
But first,—and here 's the point I fain would press,—
Don't think I 'm tattling!—
They interpose, to curb its lusciousness,
—What, 'twixt each fatling?
First comes plain bread, crisp, brown, a toasted square:
Then, a strong sage-leaf:
(So we find books with flowers dried here and there
Lest leaf engage leaf.)
First, food—then, piquancy—and last of all
Follows the thirdling:
Through wholesome hard, sharp soft, your tooth must bite
Ere reach the birdling.

Now, were there only crust to crunch, you 'd wince:
Unpalatable!
Sage-leaf is bitter-pungent—so 's a quince:
Eat each who 's able!
But through all three bite boldly—lo, the gust!
Flavor—no fixture—
Flies permeating flesh and leaf and crust
In fine admixture.
So with your meal, my poem: masticate
Sense, sight, and song there!
Digest these, and I praise your peptics' state,
Nothing found wrong there.
Whence springs my illustration who can tell?
—The more surprising
That here eggs, milk, cheese, fruit suffice so well
For gormandizing.
A fancy-freak by contrast born of thee,
Delightful Gressoney!
Who laughest "Take what is, trust what may be!"
That 's Life's true lesson,—eh?

MAISON DELAPIERRE,
Gressoney St. Jean, Val d'Aosta,
September 12, '83.

I. THE EAGLE

This poem is drawn quite closely from The Fables of Bidpai.

Dervish—(though yet un-dervished, call him so
No less beforehand: while he drudged our way,
Other his worldly name was: when he wrote
Those versicles we Persians praise him for,
—True fairy-work—Ferishtah grew his style)—
Dervish Ferishtah walked the woods one eve,
And noted on a bough a raven's nest
Whereof each youngling gaped with callow beak
Widened by want; for why? beneath the tree
Dead lay the mother-bird. "A piteous chance!
How shall they 'scape destruction?" sighed the sage
—Or sage about to be, though simple still.
Responsive to which doubt, sudden there swooped
An eagle downward, and behold he bore
(Great-hearted) in his talons flesh wherewith
He stayed their craving, then resought the sky.
"Ah, foolish, faithless me!" the observer smiled,

"Who toil and moil to eke out life, when, lo,
Providence cares for every hungry mouth!"
To profit by which lesson, home went he,
And certain days sat musing,—neither meat
Nor drink would purchase by his handiwork.
Then—for his head swam and his limbs grew faint—
Sleep overtook the unwise one, whom in dream
God thus admonished: "Hast thou marked my deed?
Which part assigned by providence dost judge
Was meant for man's example? Should he play
The helpless weakling, or the helpful strength
That captures prey and saves the perishing?
Sluggard, arise: work, eat, then feed who lack!"

Waking, "I have arisen, work I will,
Eat, and so following. Which lacks food the more,
Body or soul in me? I starve in soul:
So may mankind: and since men congregate
In towns, not woods,—to Ispahan forthwith!"

Round us the wild creatures, overhead the trees,
Underfoot the moss-tracks,—life and love with these!
I to wear a fawn-skin, thou to dress in flowers:
All the long lone summer-day, that greenwood life of ours!

Rich-pavilioned, rather,—still the world without,—
Inside—gold-roofed silk-walled silence round about!
Queen it thou on purple,—I, at watch, and ward
Couched beneath the columns, gaze, thy slave, love's guard!

So, for us no world? Let throngs press thee to me!
Up and down amid men, heart by heart fare we!
Welcome squalid vesture, harsh voice, hateful face!
God is soul, souls I and thou: with souls should souls have place.

II. THE MELON-SELLER

Going his rounds one day in Ispahan,—
Halfway on Dervishhood, not wholly there,—
Ferishtah, as he crossed a certain bridge,
Came startled on a well-remembered face.
"Can it be? What, turned melon-seller—thou?
Clad in such sordid garb, thy seat yon step
Where dogs brush by thee and express contempt?
Methinks, thy head-gear is some scooped-out gourd!

Nay, sunk to slicing up, for readier sale,
One fruit whereof the whole scarce feeds a swine?
Wast thou the Shah's Prime Minister, men saw
Ride on his right-hand while a trumpet blew
And Persia hailed the Favorite? Yea, twelve years
Are past, I judge, since that transcendency,
And thou didst peculate and art abased;
No less, twelve years since, thou didst hold in hand
Persia, couldst halve and quarter, mince its pulp
As pleased thee, and distribute—melon-like—
Portions to whoso played the parasite,
Or suck—thyself—each juicy morsel. How
Enormous thy abjection,—hell from heaven,
Made tenfold hell by contrast! Whisper me!
Dost thou curse God for granting twelve years' bliss
Only to prove this day 's the direr lot?"

Whereon the beggar raised a brow, once more
Luminous and imperial, from the rags.
"Fool, does thy folly think my foolishness
Dwells rather on the fact that God appoints
A day of woe to the unworthy one,
Than that the unworthy one, by God's award,
Tasted joy twelve years long? Or buy a slice,
Or go to school!"
To school Ferishtah went;
And, schooling ended, passed from Ispahan
To Nishapur, that Elburz looks above
—Where they dig turquoise: there kept school himself,
The melon-seller's speech, his stock in trade.
Some say a certain Jew adduced the word
Out of their book, it sounds so much the same.
אח־הטוב נקבל מאח האלהים
ואח־הדע לא נקבל : In Persian phrase,
"Shall we receive good at the hand of God
And evil not receive?" But great wits jump.

Wish no word unspoken, want no look away!
What if words were but mistake, and looks—too sudden, say!
Be unjust for once, Love! Bear it—well I may!

Do me justice always? Bid my heart—their shrine—
Render back its store of gifts, old looks and words of thine
—Oh, so all unjust—the less deserved, the more divine?

III. SHAH ABBAS

Anyhow, once full Dervish, youngsters came
To gather up his own-words, 'neath a rock
Or else a palm, by pleasant Nishapur.

Said some one, as Ferishtah paused abrupt,
Reading a certain passage from the roll
Wherein is treated of Lord Ali's life:
"Master, explain this incongruity!
When I dared question 'It is beautiful,
But is it true?'—thy answer was 'In truth
Lives beauty.' I persisting—'Beauty—yes,
In thy mind and in my mind, every mind
That apprehends: but outside—so to speak—
Did beauty live in deed as well as word,
Was this life lived, was this death died—not dreamed?'
'Many attested it for fact,' saidst thou.
'Many!' but mark, Sir! Half as long ago
As such things were,—supposing that they were,—
Reigned great Shah Abbas: he too lived and died
—How say they? Why, so strong of arm, of foot
So swift, he stayed a lion in his leap
On a stag's haunch,—with one hand grasped the stag,
With one struck down the lion: yet, no less,
Himself, that same day, feasting after sport.
Perceived a spider drop into his wine,
Let fall the flagon, died of simple fear.
So all say,—so dost thou say?"

"Wherefore not?"
Ferishtah smiled: "though strange, the story stands
Clear-chronicled: none tells it otherwise:
The fact's eye-witness bore the cup, beside."

"And dost thou credit one cup-bearer's tale,
False, very like, and futile certainly,
Yet hesitate to trust what many tongues
Combine to testify was beautiful
In deed as well as word? No fool's report,
Of lion, stag and spider, but immense
With meaning for mankind, thy race, thyself?"

Whereto the Dervish: "First amend, my son,
Thy faulty nomenclature, call belief
Belief indeed, nor grace with such a name
The easy acquiescence of mankind
In matters nowise worth dispute, since life

Lasts merely the allotted moment. Lo—
That lion-stag-and-spider tale leaves fixed
The fact for us that somewhen Abbas reigned,
Died, somehow slain,—a useful registry,—
Which therefore we—'believe'? Stand forward, thou,
My Yakub, son of Yusuf, son of Zal!
I advertise thee that our liege, the Shah
Happily regnant, hath become assured,
By opportune discovery, that thy sires,
Son by the father upwards, track their line
To—whom but that same bearer of the cup
Whose inadvertency was chargeable
With what therefrom ensued, disgust and death
To Abbas Shah, the over-nice of soul?
Whence he appoints thee,—such his clemency,—
Not death, thy due, but just a double tax
To pay, on thy particular bed of reeds
Which flower into the brush that makes a broom
Fit to sweep ceilings clear of vermin. Sure,
Thou dost believe the story nor dispute
That punishment should signalize its truth?
Down therefore with some twelve dinars! Why start,
—The stag's way with the lion hard on haunch?
'Believe the story?'—how thy words throng fast!—
'Who saw this, heard this, said this, wrote down this,
That and the other circumstance to prove
So great a prodigy surprised the world?
Needs must thou prove me fable can be fact
Or ere thou coax one piece from out my pouch!'"

"There we agree, Sir: neither of us knows,
Neither accepts that tale on evidence
Worthy to warrant the large word—belief.
Now I get near thee! Why didst pause abrupt,
Disabled by emotion at a tale
Might match—be frank!—for credibility
The figment of the spider and the cup?
—To wit, thy roll 's concerning Ali's life,
Unevidenced—thine own word! Little boots
Our sympathy with fiction! When I read
The annals and consider of Tahmasp
And that sweet sun-surpassing star his love,
I weep like a cut vine-twig, though aware
Zurah's sad fate is fiction, since the snake
He saw devour her,—how could such exist,
Having nine heads? No snake boasts more than three!
I weep, then laugh—both actions right alike.
But thou, Ferishtah, sapiency confessed,

When at the Day of Judgment God shall ask
'Didst thou believe?'—what wilt thou plead? Thy tears?
(Nay, they fell fast and stain the parchment still.)
What if thy tears meant love? Love lacking ground
—Belief,—avails thee as it would avail
My own pretence to favor since, forsooth,
I loved the lady—I who needs must laugh
To hear a snake boasts nine heads: they have three!"

"Thanks for the well-timed help that 's born, behold,
Out of thy words, my son,—belief and love!
Hast heard of Ishak son of Absal? Ay,
The very same we heard of, ten years since,
Slain in the wars: he comes back safe and sound,—
Though twenty soldiers saw him die at Yezdt,—
Just as a single mule-and-baggage boy
Declared 't was like he some day would,—for why?
The twenty soldiers lied, he saw him stout,
Cured of all wounds at once by smear of salve,
A Mubid's manufacture: such the tale.
Now, when his pair of sons were thus apprised
Effect was twofold on them. 'Hail!' crowed This:
'Dearer the news than dayspring after night!
The cure-reporting youngster warrants me
Our father shall make glad our eyes once more,
For whom, had outpoured life of mine sufficed
To bring him back, free broached were every vein!'
'Avaunt, delusive tale-concocter, news
Cruel as meteor simulating dawn!'
Whimpered the other: 'Who believes this boy,
Must disbelieve his twenty seniors: no,
Return our father shall not! Might my death
Purchase his life, how promptly would the dole
Be paid as due!' Well, ten years pass,—aha,
Ishak is marching homeward,—doubts, not he,
Are dead and done with! So, our townsfolk straight
Must take on them to counsel. 'Go thou gay,
Welcome thy father, thou of ready faith!
Hide thee, contrariwise, thou faithless one,
Expect paternal frowning, blame and blows!'
So do our townsfolk counsel: dost demur?"

"Ferishtah like those simpletons—at loss
In what is plain as pikestaff? Pish! Suppose
The trustful son had sighed 'So much the worse!
Returning means—retaking heritage
Enjoyed these ten years, who should say me nay?'
How would such trust reward him? Trustlessness

—O' the other hand—were what procured most praise
To him who judged return impossible,
Yet hated heritage procured thereby.
A fool were Ishak if he failed to prize
Mere head's work less than heart's work: no fool he!"

"Is God less wise? Resume the roll!" They did.

You groped your way across my room i' the drear dark dead of night;
At each fresh step a stumble was: but, once your lamp alight,
Easy and plain you walked again: so soon all wrong grew right!

What lay on floor to trip your foot? Each object, late awry,
Looked fitly placed, nor proved offence to footing free—for why?
The lamp showed all, discordant late, grown simple symmetry.

Be love your light and trust your guide, with these explore my
heart!
No obstacle to trip you then, strike hands and souls apart!
Since rooms and hearts are furnished so,—light shows you,—needs
love start?

IV. THE FAMILY

A certain neighbor lying sick to death,
Ferishtah grieved beneath a palm-tree, whence
He rose at peace: whereat objected one
"Gudarz our friend gasps in extremity.
Sure, thou art ignorant how close at hand
Death presses, or the cloud, which fouled so late
Thy face, had deepened down not lightened off."

"I judge there will be respite, for I prayed."

"Sir, let me understand, of charity!
Yestereve, what was thine admonishment?
'All-wise, all-good, all-mighty—God is such!'
How then should man, the all-unworthy, dare
Propose to set aside a thing ordained?
To pray means—substitute man's will for God's:
Two best wills cannot be: by consequence,
What is man bound to but—assent, say I?
Rather to rapture of thanksgiving; since
That which seems worst to man to God is best,
So, because God ordains it, best to man.

Yet man—the foolish, weak, and wicked—prays!
Urges 'My best were better, didst Thou know'!"

"List to a tale, A worthy householder
Of Shiraz had three sons, beside a spouse
Whom, cutting gourds, a serpent bit, whereon
The offended limb swelled black from foot to fork.
The husband called in aid a leech renowned
World-wide, confessed the lord of surgery,
And bade him dictate—who forthwith declared
'Sole remedy is amputation.' Straight
The husband sighed 'Thou knowest: be it so!'
His three sons heard their mother sentenced: 'Pause!'
Outbroke the elder: 'Be precipitate
Nowise, I pray thee! Take some gentler way,
Thou sage of much resource! I will not doubt
But science still may save foot, leg, and thigh!'
The next in age snapped petulant: 'Too rash!
No reason for this maiming! What, Sir Leech,
Our parent limps henceforward while we leap?
Shame on thee! Save the limb thou must and shalt!'
'Shame on yourselves, ye bold ones!' followed up
The brisk third brother, youngest, pertest too:
'The leech knows all things, we are ignorant;
What he proposes, gratefully accept!
For me, had I some unguent bound to heal
Hurts in a twinkling, hardly would I dare
Essay its virtue and so cross the sage
By cure his skill pronounces folly. Quick!
No waiting longer! There the patient lies:
Out then with implements and operate!'"

"Ah, the young devil!"

"Why, his reason chimed
Right with the Hakim's."

"Hakim's, ay—but chit's?
How? what the skilled eye saw and judged of weight
To overbear a heavy consequence,
That—shall a sciolist affect to see?
All he saw—that is, all such oaf should see,
Was just the mother's suffering."

"In my tale,
Be God the Hakim: in the husband's case,
Call ready acquiescence—aptitude
Angelic, understanding swift and sure:

Call the first son—a wise humanity,
Slow to conceive but duteous to adopt:
See in the second son—humanity,
Wrong-headed yet right-hearted, rash but kind.
Last comes the cackler of the brood, our chit
Who, aping wisdom all beyond his years,
Thinks to discard humanity itself:
Fares like the beast which should affect to fly
Because a bird with wings may spurn the ground,
So, missing heaven and losing; earth—drops how
But hell-ward? No, be man and nothing more—
Man who, as man conceiving, hopes and fears,
And craves and deprecates, and loves, and loathes,
And bids God help him, till death touch his eyes
And show God granted most, denying all."

Man I am and man would be, Love—merest man and nothing more.
Bid me seem no other! Eagles boast of pinions—let them soar!
I may put forth angel's plumage, once unmanned, but not before.

Now on earth, to stand suffices,—nay, if kneeling serves, to kneel:
Here you front me, here I find the all of heaven that earth can feel:
Sense looks straight,—not over, under,—perfect sees beyond appeal.

Good you are and wise, full circle: what to me were more outside?
Wiser wisdom, better goodness? Ah, such want the angel's wide
Sense to take and hold and keep them! Mine at least has never tried.

V. THE SUN

"And what might that bold man's announcement be"—
Ferishtah questioned—"which so moved thine ire
That thou didst curse, nay, cuff and kick—in short,
Confute the announcer? Wipe those drops away
Which start afresh upon thy face at mere
Mention of such enormity: now, speak!"

"He scrupled not to say—(thou warrantest,
O patient Sir, that I unblamed repeat
Abominable words which blister tongue?)
God once assumed on earth a human shape:
(Lo, I have spitten!) Dared I ask the grace,
Fain would I hear, of thy subtility,
From out what hole in man's corrupted heart
Creeps such a maggot: fancies verminous

Breed in the clots there, but a monster born
Of pride and folly like this pest—thyself
Only canst trace to egg-shell it hath chipped."

The sun rode high. "During our ignorance"—
Began Ferishtah—"folk esteemed as God
Yon orb: for argument, suppose him so,—
Be it the symbol, not the symbolized,
I and thou safelier take upon our lips.
Accordingly, yon orb that we adore
—What is he? Author of all light and life:
Such one must needs be somewhere: this is he.
Like what? If I may trust my human eyes,
A ball composed of spirit-fire, whence springs
—What, from this ball, my arms could circle round?
All I enjoy on earth. By consequence,
Inspiring me with—what? Why, love and praise.
I eat a palatable fig—there's love
In little: who first planted what I pluck,
Obtains my little praise, too: more of both
Keeps due proportion with more cause for each:
So, more and ever more, till most of all
Completes experience, and the orb, descried
Ultimate giver of all good, perforce
Gathers unto himself all love, all praise,
Is worshipped—which means loved and praised at height.
Back to the first good: 'twas the gardener gave
Occasion to my palate's pleasure: grace,
Plain on his part, demanded thanks on mine.
Go up above this giver,—step by step,
Gain a conception of what—(how and why,
Matters not now)—occasioned him to give,
Appointed him the gardener of the ground,—
I mount by just progression slow and sure
To some prime giver—here assumed yon orb—
Who takes my worship. Whom have I in mind,
Thus worshipping, unless a man, my like
Howe'er above me? Man, I say—how else,
I being man who worship? Here's my hand
Lifts first a mustard-seed, then weight on weight
Greater and ever greater, till at last
It lifts a melon, I suppose, then stops—
Hand-strength expended wholly: so, my love
First lauds the gardener for the fig his gift,
Then, looking higher, loves and lauds still more,
Who hires the ground, who owns the ground, Sheikh, Shah,
On and away, away and ever on,
Till, at the last, it loves and lauds the orb

Ultimate cause of all to laud and love.
Where is the break, the change of quality
In hand's power, soul's impulsion? Gift was grace,
The greatest as the smallest. Had I stopped
Anywhere in the scale, stayed love and praise
As so far only fit to follow gift,
Saying, 'I thanked the gardener for his fig,
But now that, lo, the Shah has filled my purse
With tomans which avail to purchase me
A fig-tree forest, shall I pay the same
With love and praise, the gardener's proper fee?'
Justly would whoso bears a brain object,
'Giving is giving, gift claims gift's return,
Do thou thine own part, therefore: let the Shah
Ask more from one has more to pay.' Perchance
He gave me from his treasure less by much
Than the soil's servant: let that be! My part
Is plain—to meet and match the gift and gift
With love and love, with praise and praise, till both
Cry 'All of us is thine, we can no more!'
So shall I do man's utmost—man to man:
For as our liege the Shah's sublime estate
Merely enhaloes, leaves him man the same,
So must I count that orb I call a fire
(Keep to the language of our ignorance)
Something that 's fire and more beside: mere fire
—Is it a force which, giving, knows it gives,
And wherefore, so may look for love and praise
From me, fire's like so far, however less
In all beside? Prime cause this fire shall be,
Uncaused, all-causing: hence begin the gifts,
Thither must go my love and praise—to what?
Fire? Symbol fitly serves the symbolized
Herein,—that this same object of my thanks,
While to my mind nowise conceivable
Except as mind no less than fire, refutes
Next moment mind's conception: fire is fire—
While what I needs must thank, must needs include
Purpose with power,—humanity like mine,
Imagined, for the dear necessity,
One moment in an object which the next
Confesses unimaginable. Power!
—What need of will, then? Naught opposes power:
Why, purpose? any change must be for worse:
And what occasion for beneficence
When all that is, so is and so must be?
Best being best now, change were for the worse.
Accordingly discard these qualities

Proper to imperfection, take for type
Mere fire, eject the man, retain the orb,—
The perfect and, so, inconceivable,—
And what remains to love and praise? A stone
Fair-colored proves a solace to my eye,
Rolled by my tongue brings moisture curing drouth,
And struck by steel emits a useful spark:
Shall I return it thanks, the insentient thing?
No,—man once, man forever—man in soul
As man in body: just as this can use
Its proper senses only, see and hear,
Taste, like or loathe according to its law
And not another creature's,—even so
Man's soul is moved by what, if it in turn
Must move, is kindred soul: receiving good
—Man's way—must make man's due acknowledgment,
No other, even while he reasons out
Plainly enough that, were the man unmanned,
Made angel of, angelic every way,
The love and praise that rightly seek and find
Their man-like object now,—instructed more,
Would go forth idly, air to emptiness.
Our human flower, sun-ripened, proffers scent
Though reason prove the sun lacks nose to feed
On what himself made grateful: flower and man,
Let each assume that scent and love alike
Being once born, must needs have use! Man's part
Is plain—to send love forth,—astray, perhaps:
No matter, he has done his part."

"Wherefrom
What is to follow—if I take thy sense—
But that the sun—the inconceivable
Confessed by man—comprises, all the same,
Man's every-day conception of himself—
No less remaining unconceived!"

"Agreed!"

"Yet thou, insisting on the right of man
To feel as man, not otherwise,—man, bound
By man's conditions neither less nor more,
Obliged to estimate as fair or foul,
Right, wrong, good, evil, what man's faculty
Adjudges such,—how canst thou,—plainly bound
To take man's truth for truth and only truth,—
Dare to accept, in just one case, as truth
Falsehood confessed? Flesh simulating fire—

Our fellow-man whom we his fellows know
For dust—instinct with fire unknowable!
Where 's thy man-needed truth—its proof, nay print
Of faintest passage on the tablets traced
By man, termed knowledge? 'T is conceded thee,
We lack such fancied union—fire with flesh:
But even so, to lack is not to gain
Our lack's suppliance: where 's the trace of such
Recorded?"

"What if such a tracing were?
If some strange story stood,—whate'er its worth,—
That the immensely yearned-for, once befell,
—The sun was flesh once?—(keep the figure!)"

"How?
An union inconceivable was fact?"

"Son, if the stranger have convinced himself
Fancy is fact—the sun, besides a fire,
Holds earthly substance somehow fire pervades
And yet consumes not,—earth, he understands,
With essence he remains a stranger to,—
Fitlier thou saidst 'I stand appalled before
Conception unattainable by me
Who need it most'—than this—'What? boast he holds
Conviction where I see conviction's need,
Alas,—and nothing else? then what remains
But that I straightway curse, cuff, kick the fool!'"

Fire is in the flint: true, once a spark escapes,
Fire forgets the kinship, soars till fancy shapes
Some befitting cradle where the babe had birth—
Wholly heaven 's the product, unallied to earth.
Splendors recognized as perfect in the star!—
In out flint their home was, housed as now they are.

VI. MIHRAB SHAH

Quoth an inquirer, "Praise the Merciful!
My thumb which yesterday a scorpion nipped—
(It swelled and blackened)—lo, is sound again!
By application of a virtuous root
The burning has abated: that is well.
But now methinks I have a mind to ask,—

Since this discomfort came of culling herbs
Nor meaning harm,—why needs a scorpion be?
Yea, there began, from when my thumb last throbbed,
Advance in question-framing, till I asked
Wherefore should any evil hap to man—
From ache of flesh to agony of soul—
Since God's All-mercy mates All-potency?
Nay, why permits he evil to himself—
Man's sin, accounted such? Suppose a world
Purged of all pain, with fit inhabitant—
Man pure of evil in thought, word, and deed—
Were it not well? Then, wherefore otherwise?
Too good result? But he is wholly good!
Hard to effect? Ay, were he impotent!
Teach me, Ferishtah!"

Said the Dervish: "Friend,
My chance, escaped to-day, was worse than thine:
I, as I woke this morning, raised my head,
Which never tumbled but stuck fast on neck.
Was not I glad and thankful!"

"How could head
Tumble from neck, unchopped—inform me first!
Unless we take Firdausi's tale for truth,
Who ever heard the like?"

"The like might hap
By natural law: I let my staff fall thus—
It goes to ground, I know not why. Suppose,
Whene'er my hold was loosed, it skyward sprang
As certainly, and all experience proved
That, just as staves when unsupported sink,
So, unconfined, they soar?"

"Let such be law—
Why, a new chapter of sad accidents
Were added to humanity's mischance,
No doubt at all, and as a man's false step
Now lays him prone on earth, contrariwise,
Removal from his shoulder o£ a weight
Might start him upwards to perdition. Ay!
But, since such law exists in just thy brain,
I shall not hesitate to doff my cap
For fear my head take flight."

"Nor feel relief
Finding it firm on shoulder. Tell me, now!

What were the bond 'twixt man and man, dost judge,
Pain once abolished? Come, be true! Our Shah—
How stands he in thy favor? Why that shrug?
Is not he lord and ruler?"

"Easily!
His mother bore him, first of those four wives
Provided by his father, such his luck:
Since when his business simply was to breathe
And take each day's new bounty. There he stands—
Where else had I stood, were his birth-star mine?
No, to respect men's power, I needs must see
Men's bare hands seek, find, grasp and wield the sword
Nobody else can brandish! Bless his heart,
'Tis said, he scarcely counts his fingers right!"

"Well, then—his princely doles! from every feast
Off go the feasted with the dish they ate
And cup they drank from,—nay, a change besides
Of garments" ...

"Sir, put case, for service done,—
Or best, for love's sake,—such and such a slave
Sold his allowance of sour lentil-soup
To herewith purchase me a pipe-stick,—nay,
If he, by but one hour, cut short his sleep
To clout my shoe,—that were a sacrifice!"

"All praise his gracious bearing."

"All praise mine—
Or would praise did they never make approach
Except on all-fours, crawling till I bade,
'Now that with eyelids thou hast touched the earth,
Come close and have no fear, poor nothingness!'
What wonder that the lady-rose I woo
And palisade about from every wind,
Holds herself handsomely? The wilding, now,
Ruffled outside at pleasure of the blast,
That still lifts up with something of a smile
Its poor attempt at bloom" ...

"A blameless life,
Where wrong might revel with impunity—
Remember that!"

"The falcon on his fist—
Reclaimed and trained and belled and beautified

Till she believes herself the Simorgh's match—
She only deigns destroy the antelope,
Stoops at no carrion-crow: thou marvellest?

"So be it, then! He wakes no love in thee
For any one of divers attributes
Commonly deemed love-worthy. All the same,
I would he were not wasting, slow but sure,
With that internal ulcer" ...

"Say'st thou so?
How should I guess? Alack, poor soul! But stay—
Sure in the reach of art some remedy
Must lie to hand: or if it lurk,—that leech
Of fame in Tebriz, why not seek his aid?
Couldst not thou, Dervish, counsel in the case?"

"My counsel might be—what imports a pang
The more or less, which puts an end to one
Odious in spite of every attribute
Commonly deemed love-worthy?"

"Attributes?
Faugh!—nay, Ferishtah,—'tis an ulcer, think!
Attributes, quotha? Here 's poor flesh and blood,
Like thine and mine and every man's, a prey
To hell-fire! Hast thou lost thy wits for once?"

"Friend, here they are to find and profit by!
Put pain from out the world, what room were left
For thanks to God, for love to Man? Why thanks,—
Except for some escape, whatever the style,
From pain that might be, name it as thou mayst?
Why love,—when all thy kind, save me, suppose,
Thy father, and thy son, and ... well, thy dog,
To eke the decent number out—we few
Who happen—like a handful of chance stars
From the unnumbered host—to shine o'erhead
And lend thee light,—our twinkle all thy store,—
We only take thy love! Mankind, forsooth?
Who sympathizes with their general joy
Foolish as undeserved? But pain—see God's
Wisdom at work!—man's heart is made to judge
Pain deserved nowhere by the common flesh
Our birthright,—bad and good deserve alike
No pain, to human apprehension! Lust,
Greed, cruelty, injustice crave (we hold)
Due punishment from somebody, no doubt:

But ulcer in the midriff! that brings flesh
Triumphant from the bar whereto arraigned
Soul quakes with reason. In the eye of God
Pain may have purpose and be justified:
Man's sense avails to only see, in pain,
A hateful chance no man but would avert
Or, failing, needs must pity. Thanks to God
And love to man,—from man take these away,
And what is man worth? Therefore, Mihrab Shah,
Tax me my bread and salt twice over, claim
Laila my daughter for thy sport,—go on!
Slay my son's self, maintain thy poetry
Beats mine,—thou meritest a dozen deaths!
But—ulcer in the stomach,—ah, poor soul,
Try a fig-plaster: may it ease thy pangs!"

So, the head aches and the limbs are faint!
Flesh is a burden—even to you!
Can I force a smile with a fancy quaint?
Why are my ailments none or few?

In the soul of me sits sluggishness;
Body so strong and will so weak:
The slave stands fit for the labor—yes,
But the master's mandate is still to seek.

You, now—what if the outside clay
Helped, not hindered the inside flame?
My dim to-morrow—your plain to-day,
Yours the achievement, mine the aim?

So were it rightly, so shall it be!
Only, while earth we pace together
For the purpose apportioned you and me,
Closer we tread for a common tether.

You shall sigh, "Wait for his sluggish soul!
Shame he should lag, not lamed as I!"
May not I smile, "Ungained her goal:
Body may reach her—by and by"?

VII. A CAMEL-DRIVER

"How of his fate, the Pilgrims' soldier-guide
Condemned" (Ferishtah questioned), "for he slew

The merchant whom he convoyed with his bales
—A special treachery?"

"Sir, the proofs were plain:
Justice was satisfied: between two boards
The rogue was sawn asunder, rightly served."

"With all wise men's approval—mine at least."

"Himself, indeed, confessed as much. 'I die
Justly' (groaned he) 'through over-greediness
Which tempted me to rob: but grieve the most
That he who quickened sin at slumber,—ay,
Prompted and pestered me till thought grew deed,—
The same is fled to Syria and is safe,
Laughing at me thus left to pay for both.
My comfort is that God reserves for him
Hell's hottest'" ...

"Idle words."

"Enlighten me!
Wherefore so idle? Punishment by man
Has thy assent,—the word is on thy lips.
By parity of reason, punishment
By God should likelier win thy thanks and praise."

"Man acts as man must: God, as God beseems.
A camel-driver, when his beast will bite,
Thumps her athwart the muzzle; why?"

"How else
Instruct the creature—mouths should munch not bite?"

"True, he is man, knows but man's trick to teach.
Suppose some plain word, told her first of all,
Had hindered any biting?"

"Find him such,
And fit the beast with understanding first!
No understanding animals like Rakhsh
Nowadays, Master! Till they breed on earth,
For teaching—blows must serve."

"Who deals the blow—
What if by some rare method,—magic, say,—
He saw into the biter's very soul,
And knew the fault was so repented of

It could not happen twice?"

"That 's something: still,
I hear, methinks, the driver say, 'No less
Take thy fault's due! Those long-necked sisters, see,
Lean all a-stretch to know if biting meets
Punishment or enjoys impunity.
For their sakes—thwack!'"

"The journey home at end,
The solitary beast safe-stabled now,
In comes the driver to avenge a wrong
Suffered from six months since,—apparently
With patience, nay, approval: when the jaws
Met i' the small o' the arm. 'Ha, Ladykin,
Still at thy frolics, girl of gold?' laughed he:
'Eat flesh? Rye-grass content thee rather with,
Whereof accept a bundle!' Now,—what change!
Laughter by no means! Now 't is, 'Fiend, thy frisk
Was fit to find thee provender, didst judge?
Behold this red-hot twy-prong, thus I stick
To hiss i' the soft of thee!'"

"Behold? behold
A crazy noddle, rather! Sure the brute
Might wellnigh have plain speech coaxed out of tongue,
And grow as voluble as Rakhsh himself
At such mad outrage. 'Could I take thy mind,
Guess thy desire? If biting was offence,
Wherefore the rye-grass bundle, why each day's
Patting and petting, but to intimate
My playsomeness had pleased thee? Thou endowed
With reason, truly!'"

"Reason aims to raise
Some makeshift scaffold-vantage midway, whence
Man dares, for life's brief moment, peer below:
But ape omniscience? Nay! The ladder lent
To climb by, step and step, until we reach
The little foothold-rise allowed mankind
To mount on and thence guess the sun's survey—
Shall this avail to show us world-wide truth
Stretched for the sun's descrying? Reason bids,
'Teach, Man, thy beast his duty first of all
Or last of all, with blows if blows must be,—
How else accomplish teaching?' Reason adds,
'Before man's First, and after man's poor Last,
God operated and will operate.'

—Process of which man merely knows this much,—
That nowise it resembles man's at all,
Teaching or punishing."

"It follows, then,
That any malefactor I would smite
With God's allowance, God himself will spare
Presumably. No scapegrace? Then, rejoice
Thou snatch-grace safe in Syria!"

"Friend, such view
Is but man's-wonderful and wide mistake.
Man lumps his kind i' the mass: God singles thence
Unit by unit. Thou and God exist—
So think!—for certain: think the mass—mankind—
Disparts, disperses, leaves thyself alone!
Ask thy lone soul what laws are plain to thee,—
Thee and no other,—stand or fall by them!
That is the part for thee: regard all else
For what it may be—Time's illusion. This
Be sure of—ignorance that sins, is safe.
No punishment like knowledge! Instance, now!
My father's choicest treasure was a book
Wherein he, day by day and year by year,
Recorded gains of wisdom for my sake
When I should grow to manhood. While a child,
Coming upon the casket where it lay
Unguarded,—-what did I but toss the thing
Into a fire to make more flame therewith,
Meaning no harm? So acts man three-years-old!
I grieve now at my loss by witlessness,
But guilt was none to punish. Man mature—
Each word of his I lightly held, each look
I turned from—wish that wished in vain—nay, will
That willed and yet went all to waste—'t is these
Rankle like fire. Forgiveness? rather grant
Forgetfulness! The past is past and lost.
However near I stand in his regard,
So much the nearer had I stood by steps
Offered the feet which rashly spurned their help
That I call Hell; why further punishment?"

When I vexed you and you chid me,
And I owned my fault and turned
My cheek the way you bid me,
And confessed the blow well earned,—

My comfort all the while was
—Fault was faulty—near, not quite!
Do you wonder why the smile was?
O'erpunished wrong grew right.

But faults, you ne'er suspected,
Nay, praised, no faults at all,—
Those would you had detected—
Crushed eggs whence snakes could crawl!

VIII. TWO CAMELS

Quoth one: "Sir, solve a scruple! No true sage
I hear of, but instructs his scholar thus:
'Wouldst thou be wise? Then mortify thyself!
Balk of its craving every bestial sense!
Say, "If I relish melons—so do swine!
Horse, ass, and mule consume their provender
Nor leave a pea-pod: fasting feeds the soul."'
Thus they admonish: while thyself, I note,
Eatest thy ration with an appetite,
Nor fallest foul of whoso licks his lips
And sighs—'Well-saffroned was that barley-soup!'
Can wisdom coexist with—gorge-and-swill,
I say not,—simply sensual preference
For this or that fantastic meat and drink?
Moreover, wind blows sharper than its wont
This morning, and thou hast already donned
Thy sheepskin over-garment: sure the sage
Is busied with conceits that soar above
A petty change of season and its chance
Of causing ordinary flesh to sneeze?
I always thought, Sir" ...

"Son," Ferishtah said,
"Truth ought to seem as never thought before.
How if I give it birth in parable?
A neighbor owns two camels, beasts of price
And promise, destined each to go, next week,
Swiftly and surely with his merchandise
From Nishapur to Sebzevar, no truce
To tramp, but travel, spite of sands and drouth,
In days so many, lest they miss the Fair.
Each falls to meditation o'er his crib
Piled high with provender before the start.
Quoth this: 'My soul is set on winning praise

From goodman lord and master,—hump to hoof,
I dedicate me to his service. How?
Grass, purslane, lupines, and I know not what,
Crammed in my manger? Ha, I see—I see!
No, master, spare thy money! I shall trudge
The distance and yet cost thee not a doit
Beyond my supper on this mouldy bran.'
'Be magnified, O master, for the meal
So opportunely liberal!' quoth that.
'What use of strength in me but to surmount
Sands and simooms, and bend beneath thy bales
No knee until I reach the glad bazaar?
Thus I do justice to thy fare: no sprig
Of toothsome chervil must I leave unchewed!
Too bitterly should I reproach myself
Did I sink down in sight of Sebzevar,
Remembering how the merest mouthful more
Had heartened me to manage yet a mile!'
And so it proved: the too-abstemious brute
Midway broke down, his pack rejoiced the thieves,
His carcass fed the vultures: not so he
The wisely thankful, who, good market-drudge,
Let down his lading in the market-place,
No damage to a single pack. Which beast,
Think ye, had praise and patting and a brand
Of good-and-faithful-servant fixed on flank?
So, with thy squeamish scruple. What imports
Fasting or feasting? Do thy day's work, dare
Refuse no help thereto, since help refused
Is hindrance sought and found. Win but the race—
Who shall object 'He tossed three wine-cups off,
And, just at starting, Lilith kissed his lips'?

"More soberly,—consider this, my Son!
Put case I never have myself enjoyed,
Known by experience what enjoyment means,
How shall I—share enjoyment?—no, indeed!—
Supply it to my fellows,—ignorant,
As so I should be of the thing they crave,
How it affects them, works for good or ill.
Style my enjoyment self-indulgence—sin—
Why should I labor to infect my kind
With sin's occasion, bid them too enjoy,
Who else might neither catch nor give again
Joy's plague, but live in righteous misery?
Just as I cannot, till myself convinced,
Impart conviction, so, to deal forth joy
Adroitly, needs must I know joy myself.

Renounce joy for my fellows' sake? That 's joy
Beyond joy; but renounced for mine, not theirs?
Why, the physician called to help the sick,
Cries 'Let me, first of all, discard my health!'
No, Son: the richness hearted in such joy
Is in the knowing what are gifts we give,
Not in a vain endeavor not to know!
Therefore, desire joy and thank God for it!
The Adversary said,—a Jew reports,—
: החנם רא איוב אלהים
In Persian phrase, 'Does Job fear God for naught?'
Job's creatureship is not abjured, thou fool!
He nowise isolates himself and plays
The independent equal, owns no more
Than himself gave himself, so why thank God?
A proper speech were this מאלהים
'Equals we are, Job, labor for thyself,
Nor bid me help thee: bear, as best flesh may,
Pains I inflict not nor avail to cure:
Beg of me nothing thou thyself mayst win
By work, or waive with magnanimity,
Since we are peers acknowledged,—scarcely peers,
Had I implanted any want of thine
Only my power could meet and gratify.'
No: rather hear, at man's indifference—
'Wherefore did I contrive for thee that ear
Hungry for music, and direct thine eye
To where I hold a seven-stringed instrument,
Unless I meant thee to beseech me play?'"

Once I saw a chemist take a pinch of powder
—Simple dust it seemed—and half-unstop a phial:
—Out dropped harmless dew. "Mixed nothings make" (quoth he)
"Something!" So they did: a thunderclap, but louder—
Lightning-flash, but fiercer—put spectators' nerves to trial:
Sure enough, we learned what was, imagined what might be.

Had I no experience how a lip's mere tremble,
Look's half hesitation, cheek's just change of color,
These effect a heartquake,—how should I conceive
What a heaven there may be? Let it but resemble
Earth myself have known! No bliss that's finer, fuller,
Only—bliss that lasts, they say, and fain would I believe.

IX. CHERRIES

"What, I disturb thee at thy morning-meal:
Cherries so ripe already? Eat apace!
I recollect thy lesson yesterday.
Yet—thanks, Sir, for thy leave to interrupt" ...

"Friend, I have finished my repast, thank God!"

"There now, thy thanks for breaking fast on fruit!—
Thanks being praise, or tantamount thereto.
Prithee consider, have not things degree,
Lofty and low? Are things not great and small.
Thence claiming praise and wonder more or less?
Shall we confuse them, with thy warrant too,
Whose doctrine otherwise begins and ends
With just this precept, 'Never faith enough
In man as weakness, God as potency'?
When I would pay soul's tribute to that same,
Why not look up in wonder, bid the stars
Attest my praise of the All-mighty One?
What are man's puny members and as mean
Requirements weighed with Star-King Mushtari?
There is the marvel!"

"Not to man—that 's me.
List to what happened late, in fact or dream.
A certain stranger, bound from far away,
Still the Shah's subject, found himself before
Ispahan palace-gate. As duty bade,
He enters in the courts, will, if he may,
See so much glory as befits a slave
Who only comes, of mind to testify
How great and good is shown our lord the Shah.
In he walks, round he casts his eye about,
Looks up and down, admires to heart's content,
Ascends the gallery, tries door and door,
None says his reverence nay: peeps in at each,
Wonders at all the unimagined use,
Gold here and jewels there,—so vast, that hall—
So perfect yon pavilion!—lamps above
Bidding look up from luxuries below,—
Evermore wonder topping wonder,—last—
Sudden he comes upon a cosy nook,
A nest-like little chamber, with his name,
His own, yea, his and no mistake at all,
Plain o'er the entry,—what, and he descries
Just those arrangements inside,—oh, the care!—
Suited to soul and body both,—so snug

The cushion—nay, the pipe-stand furnished so!
Whereat he cries aloud,—what think'st thou, Friend?
'That these my slippers should be just my choice,
Even to the color that I most affect,
Is nothing: ah, that lamp, the central sun,
What must it light within its minaret
I scarce dare guess the good of! Who lives there?
That let me wonder at,—no slipper toys
Meant for the foot, forsooth, which kicks them—thus!'

"Never enough faith in omnipotence,—
Never too much, by parity, of faith
In impuissance, man's—which turns to strength
When once acknowledged weakness every way.
How? Hear the teaching of another tale.

"Two men once owed the Shah a mighty sum,
Beggars they both were: this one crossed his arms
And bowed his head,—'whereof,' sighed he, 'each hair
Proved it a jewel, how the host's amount
Were idly strewn for payment at thy feet!'

'Lord, here they lie, my havings poor and scant!
All of the berries on my currant-bush,
What roots of garlic have escaped the mice,
And some five pippins from the seedling tree,—
Would they were half-a-dozen! Anyhow,
Accept my all, poor beggar that I am!'
'Received in full of all demands!' smiled back
The apportioner of every lot of ground
From inch to acre. Littleness of love
Befits the littleness of loving thing.
What if he boasted 'Seeing I am great,
Great must my corresponding tribute be'?
Mushtari,—well, suppose him seven times seven
The sun's superior, proved so by some sage:
Am I that sage? To me his twinkle blue
Is all I know of him and thank him for,
And therefore I have put the same in verse—
'Like yon blue twinkle, twinks thine eye, my Love!'

Neither shalt thou be troubled overmuch
Because thy offering—littleness itself—
Is lessened by admixture sad and strange
Of mere man's motives,—praise with fear, and love
With looking after that same love's reward.
Alas, Friend, what was free from this alloy,—
Some smatch thereof,—in best and purest love

Proffered thy earthly father? Dust thou art,
Dust shalt be to the end. Thy father took
The dust, and kindly called the handful—gold,
Nor cared to count what sparkled here and there
Sagely unanalytic. Thank, praise, love
(Sum up thus) for the lowest favors first,
The commonest of comforts! aught beside
Very omnipotence had overlooked
Such needs, arranging for thy little life.
Nor waste thy power of love in wonderment
At what thou wiselier lettest shine unsoiled
By breath of word. That this last cherry soothes
A roughness of my palate, that I know:
His Maker knows why Mushtari was made."

Verse-making was least of my virtues: I viewed with despair
Wealth that never yet was but might be—all that verse-making were
If the life would but lengthen to wish, let the mind be laid bare.
So I said "To do little is bad, to do nothing is worse"—
And made verse.

Love-making,—how simple a matter! No depths to explore,
No heights in a life to ascend! No disheartening Before,
No affrighting Hereafter,—love now will be love evermore.
So I felt "To keep silence were folly:"—all language above,
I made love.

X. PLOT-CULTURE

"Ay, but, Ferishtah,"—a disciple smirked,—
"That verse of thine 'How twinks thine eye, my Love,
Blue as yon star-beam!' much arrides myself
Who haply may obtain a kiss therewith
This eve from Laila where the palms abound—
My youth, my warrant—so the palms be close!
Suppose when thou art earnest in discourse
Concerning high and holy things,—abrupt
I out with—'Laila's lip, how honey-sweet!'—
What say'st thou, were it scandalous or no?
I feel thy shoe sent flying at my mouth
For daring—prodigy of impudence—
Publish what, secret, were permissible.
Well,—one slide further in the imagined slough,—
Knee-deep therein, (respect thy reverence!)—
Suppose me well aware thy very self

Stooped prying through the palm-screen, while I dared
Solace me with caressings all the same?
Unutterable, nay—unthinkable,
Undreamable a deed of shame! Alack,
How will it fare shouldst thou impress on me
That certainly an Eye is over all
And each, to mark the minute's deed, word, thought,
As worthy of reward or punishment?
Shall I permit my sense an Eye-viewed shame,
Broad daylight perpetration,—so to speak,—
I had not dared to breathe within the Ear,
With black night's help about me? Yet I stand
A man, no monster, made of flesh not cloud:
Why made so, if my making prove offence
To Maker's eye and ear?"

"Thou wouldst not stand
Distinctly Man,"—Ferishtah made reply,
"Not the mere creature,—did no limit-line
Round thee about, apportion thee thy place
Clean-cut from out and off the illimitable,—
Minuteness severed from immensity.
All of thee for the Maker,—for thyself,
Workings inside the circle that evolve
Thine all,—the product of thy cultured plot.
So much of grain the ground's lord bids thee yield:
Bring sacks to granary in Autumn! spare
Daily intelligence of this manure,
That compost, how they tend to feed the soil:
There thou art master sole and absolute
—Only, remember doomsday! Twit'st thou me
Because I turn away my outraged nose
Shouldst thou obtrude thereon a shovelful
Of fertilizing kisses? Since thy sire
Wills and obtains thy marriage with the maid,
Enough! Be reticent, I counsel thee,
Nor venture to acquaint him, point by point,
What he procures thee. Is he so obtuse?
Keep thy instruction to thyself! My ass—
Only from him expect acknowledgment,
The while he champs my gift, a thistle-bunch,
How much he loves the largess: of his love
I only tolerate so much as tells
By wrinkling nose and inarticulate grunt,
The meal, that heartens him to do my work,
Tickles his palate as I meant it should."

Not with my Soul, Love!—bid no soul like mine
Lap thee around nor leave the poor Sense room!
Soul,—travel-worn, toil-weary,—would confine
Along with Soul, Soul's gains from glow and gloom,
Captures from soarings high and divings deep.
Spoil-laden Soul, how should such memories sleep?
Take Sense, too—let me love entire and whole—
Not with my Soul!

Eyes shall meet eyes and find no eyes between,
Lips feed on lips, no other lips to fear!
No past, no future—so thine arms but screen
The present from surprise! not there, 't is here—
Not then, 't is now:—back, memories that intrude!
Make, Love, the universe our solitude,
And, over all the rest, oblivion roll—
Sense quenching Soul!

XI. A PILLAR AT SEBZEVAR

"Knowledge deposed, then!"—groaned whom that most grieved
As foolishest of all the company.
"What, knowledge, man's distinctive attribute,
He doffs that crown to emulate an ass
Because the unknowing long-ears loves at least
Husked lupines, and belike the feeder's self
—Whose purpose in the dole what ass divines?"

"Friend," quoth Ferishtah, "all I seem to know
Is—I know nothing save that love I can
Boundlessly, endlessly. My curls were crowned
In youth with knowledge,—off, alas, crown slipped
Next moment, pushed by better knowledge still
Which nowise proved more constant: gain, to-day,
Was toppling loss to-morrow, lay at last
—Knowledge, the golden?—lacquered ignorance!
As gain—mistrust it! Not as means to gain:
Lacquer we learn by: cast in fining-pot,
We learn, when what seemed ore assayed proves dross,—
Surelier true gold's worth, guess how purity
I' the lode were precious could one light on ore
Clarified up to test of crucible.
The prize is in the process: knowledge means
Ever-renewed assurance by defeat
That victory is somehow still to reach,
But love is victory, the prize itself:

Love—trust to! Be rewarded for the trust
In trust's mere act. In love success is sure,
Attainment—no delusion, whatsoe'er
The prize be: apprehended as a prize,
A prize it is. Thy child as surely grasps
An orange as he fails to grasp the sun
Assumed his capture. What if soon he finds
The foolish fruit unworthy grasping? Joy
In shape and color,—that was joy as true—
Worthy in its degree of love—as grasp
Of sun were, which had singed his hand beside.
What if he said the orange held no juice
Since it was not that sun he hoped to suck?
This constitutes the curse that spoils our life
And sets man maundering of his misery,
That there 's no meanest atom he obtains
Of what he counts for knowledge but he cries
'Hold here,—I have the whole thing,—know, this time,
Nor need search farther!' Whereas, strew his path
With pleasures, and he scorns them while he stoops:
'This fitly call'st thou pleasure, pick up this
And praise it, truly? I reserve my thanks
For something more substantial.' Fool not thus
In practising with life and its delights!
Enjoy the present gift, nor wait to know
The unknowable. Enough to say 'I feel
Love's sure effect, and, being loved, must love
The love its cause behind,—I can and do!'
Nor turn to try thy brain-power on the fact,
(Apart from as it strikes thee, here and now—
Its how and why, i' the future and elsewhere)
Except to—yet once more, and ever again,
Confirm thee in thy utter ignorance:
Assured that, whatsoe'er the quality
Of love's cause, save that love was caused thereby,
This—nigh upon revealment as it seemed
A minute since—defies thy longing looks,
Withdrawn into the unknowable once more.
Wholly distrust thy knowledge, then, and trust
As wholly love allied to ignorance!
There lies thy truth and safety. Love is praise,
And praise is love! Refine the same, contrive
An intellectual tribute—ignorance
Appreciating ere approbative
Of knowledge that is infinite? With us,
The small, who use the knowledge of our kind
Greater than we, more wisely ignorance
Restricts its apprehension, sees and knows

No more than brain accepts in faith of sight,
Takes first what comes first, only sure so far.
By Sebzevar a certain pillar stands
So aptly that its gnomon tells the hour;
What if the townsmen said 'Before we thank
Who placed it, for his serviceable craft,
And go to dinner since its shade tells noon,
Needs must we have the craftsman's purpose clear
On half a hundred more recondite points
Than a mere summons to a vulgar meal!'
Better they say 'How opportune the help!
Be loved and praised, thou kindly-hearted sage
Whom Hudhud taught,—the gracious spirit-bird,—
How to construct the pillar, teach the time!'
So let us say—not 'Since we know, we love,'
But rather 'Since we love, we know enough.'
Perhaps the pillar by a spell controlled
Mushtari in his courses? Added grace
Surely I count it that the sage devised,
Beside celestial service, ministry
To all the land, by one sharp shade at noon
Falling as folk foresee. Once more, then, Friend—
(What ever in those careless ears of thine
Withal I needs must round thee)—knowledge doubt
Even wherein it seems demonstrable!
Love,—in the claim for love, that 's gratitude
For apprehended pleasure, nowise doubt!
Pay its due tribute,—sure that pleasure is,
While knowledge may be, at the most. See, now!
Eating my breakfast, I thanked God.—'For love
Shown in the cherries' flavor? Consecrate
So petty an example?' There 's the fault!
We circumscribe omnipotence. Search sand
To unearth water: if first handful scooped
Yields thee a draught, what need of digging down
Full fifty fathoms deep to find a spring
Whereof the pulse might deluge half the land?
Drain the sufficient drop, and praise what checks
The drouth that glues thy tongue,—what more would help
A brimful cistern? Ask the cistern's boon
When thou wouldst solace camels: in thy case,
Relish the drop and love the lovable!"

"And what may be unlovable?"

"Why, hate!
If out of sand comes sand and naught but sand,
Affect not to be quaffing at mirage,

Nor nickname pain as pleasure. That, belike,
Constitutes just the trial of thy wit
And worthiness to gain promotion,—hence,
Proves the true purpose of thine actual life.
Thy soul's environment of things perceived,
Things visible and things invisible,
Fact, fancy—all was purposed to evolve
This and this only—was thy wit of worth
To recognize the drop's use, love the same,
And loyally declare against mirage
Though all the world asseverated dust
Was good to drink? Say, 'what made moist my lip,
That I acknowledged moisture:' thou art saved!

For why? The creature and creator stand
Rightly related so. Consider well!
Were knowledge all thy faculty, then God
Must be ignored: love gains him by first leap.
Frankly accept the creatureship: ask good
To love for: press bold to the tether's end
Allotted to this life's intelligence!
'So we offend?' Will it offend thyself
If—impuissance praying potency—
Thy child beseech that thou command the sun
Rise bright to-morrow—thou, he thinks supreme
In power and goodness, why shouldst thou refuse?
Afterward, when the child matures, perchance
The fault were greater if, with wit full-grown,
The stripling dared to ask for a dinar,
Than that the boy cried 'Pluck Sitara down
And give her me to play with!' 'T is for him
To have no bounds to his belief in thee:
For thee it also is to let her shine
Lustrous and lonely, so best serving him!"

Ask not one least word of praise!
Words declare your eyes are bright?
What then meant that summer day's
Silence spent in one long gaze?
Was my silence wrong or right?

Words of praise were all to seek!
Face of you and form of you,
Did they find the praise so weak
When my lips just touched your cheek—
Touch which let my soul come through?

"Look, I strew beans" ...

(Ferishtah, we premise,
Strove this way with a scholar's cavilment
Who put the peevish question: "Sir, be frank!
A good thing or a bad thing—Life is which?
Shine and shade, happiness and misery
Battle it out there: which force beats, I ask?
If I pick beans from out a bushelful—
This one, this other,—then demand of thee
What color names each justly in the main,—
'Black' I expect, and 'White' ensues reply:
No hesitation for what speck, spot, splash
Of either color's opposite, intrudes
To modify thy judgment. Well, for beans
Substitute days,—show, ranged in order, Life—
Then, tell me its true color! Time is short,
Life's days compose a span,—as brief be speech!
Black I pronounce for, like the Indian Sage,—
Black—present, past, and future, interspersed
With blanks, no doubt, which simple folk style Good
Because not Evil: no, indeed? Forsooth,
Black's shade on White is White too! What's the worst
Of Evil but that, past, it overshades
The else-exempted, present?—memory,
We call the plague! 'Nay, but our memory fades
And leaves the past unsullied!' Does it so?
Why, straight the purpose of such breathing-space,
Such respite from past ills, grows plain enough!
What follows on remembrance of the past?
Fear of the future! Life, from birth to death,
Means—either looking back on harm escaped,
Or looking forward to that harm's return
With tenfold power of harming. Black, not White,
Never the whole consummate quietude
Life should be, troubled by no fear!—nor hope—
I 'll say, since lamplight dies in noontide, hope
Loses itself in certainty. Such lot
Man's might have been: I leave the consequence
To bolder critics or the Primal Cause;
Such am not I: but, man—as man I speak:
Black is the bean-throw: evil is the Life!")

"Look, I strew beans,"—resumed Ferishtah,—"beans

Blackish and whitish; what they figure forth
Shall be man's sum of moments, bad and good,
That make up Life,—each moment when he feels
Pleasure or pain, his poorest fact of sense,
Consciousness anyhow: there 's stand the first;
Whence next advance shall be from points to line,
Singulars to a series, parts to whole,
And moments to the Life. How look they now,
Viewed in the large, those little joys and griefs
Ranged duly all a-row at last, like beans
—These which I strew? This bean was white, this—black,
Set by itself,—but see if good and bad
Each following either in companionship,
Black have not grown less black and white less white,
Till blackish seems but dun, and whitish—gray,
And the whole line turns—well, or black to thee
Or white belike to me—no matter which:
The main result is—both are modified
According to our eye's scope, power of range
Before and after. Black dost call this bean?
What, with a whiteness in its wake, which—see—
Suffuses half its neighbor?—and, in turn,
Lowers its pearliness late absolute,
Frowned upon by the jet which follows hard—
Else wholly white my bean were. Choose a joy!
Bettered it was by sorrow gone before,
And sobered somewhat by the shadowy sense
Of sorrow which came after or might come.
Joy, sorrow,—by precedence, subsequence—
Either on each, make fusion, mix in Life
That 's both and neither wholly: gray or dun?
Dun thou decidest? gray prevails, say I:
Wherefore? Because my view is wide enough,
Reaches from first to last nor winks at all:
Motion achieves it: stop short—fast we stick,—
Probably at the bean that 's blackest.

"Since—
Son, trust me,—this I know and only this—
I am in motion, and all things beside
That circle round my passage through their midst,—
Motionless, these are, as regarding me:
—Which means, myself I solely recognize.
They too may recognize themselves, not me,
For aught I know or care: but plain they serve
This, if no other purpose—stuff to try
And test my power upon of raying light
And lending hue to all things as I go

Moonlike through vapor. Mark the flying orb!
Think'st thou the halo, painted still afresh
At each new cloud-fleece pierced and passaged through,
This was and is and will be evermore
Colored in permanence? The glory swims
Girdling the glory-giver, swallowed straight
By night's abysmal gloom, unglorified
Behind as erst before the advancer: gloom?
Faced by the onward-faring, see, succeeds
From the abandoned heaven a next surprise,
And where 's the gloom now?—silver-smitten straight,
One glow and variegation! So with me,
Who move and make—myself—the black, the white,
The good, the bad, of life's environment.
Stand still! black stays black: start again! there 's white
Asserts supremacy: the motion 's all
That colors me my moment: seen as joy?—
I have escaped from sorrow, or that was
Or might have been: as sorrow?—thence shall be
Escape as certain: white preceded black,
Black shall give way to white as duly,—so,
Deepest in black means white most imminent,
Stand still,—have no before, no after!—life
Proves death, existence grows impossible
To man like me. 'What else is blessed sleep
But death, then?' Why, a rapture of release
From toil,—that 's sleep's approach: as certainly,
The end of sleep means, toil is triumphed o'er:
These round the blank inconsciousness between
Brightness and brightness, either pushed to blaze
Just through that blank's interposition. Hence
The use of things external: man—that 's I—
Practise thereon my power of casting light,
And calling substance,—when the light I cast
Breaks into color,—by its proper name
—A truth and yet a falsity: black, white,
Names each bean taken from what lay so close
And threw such tint: pain might mean pain indeed
Seen in the passage past it,—pleasure prove
No mere delusion while I pause to look,—
Though what an idle fancy was that fear
Which overhung and hindered pleasure's hue!
While how, again, pain's shade enhanced the shine
Of pleasure, else no pleasure! Such effects
Came of such causes. Passage at an end,—
Past, present, future pains and pleasures fused
So that one glance may gather blacks and whites
Into a lifetime,—like my bean-streak there,

Why, white they whirl into, not black—for me!"

"Ay, but for me? The indubitable blacks,
Immeasurable miseries, here, there
And everywhere i' the world—world outside thine
Paled off so opportunely,—body's plague,
Torment of soul,—where 's found thy fellowship
With wide humanity all round about
Reeling beneath its burden? What 's despair?
Behold that man, that woman, child—nay, brute!
Will any speck of white unblacken life
Splashed, splotched, dyed hell-deep now from end to end
For him or her or it—who knows? Not I!"

"Nor I, Son! 'It' shall stand for bird, beast, fish,
Reptile, and insect even: take the last!
There 's the palm-aphis, minute miracle
As wondrous every whit as thou or I:
Well, and his world's the palm-frond, there he 's born,
Lives, breeds, and dies in that circumference,
An inch of green for cradle, pasture-ground,
Purlieu and grave: the palm's use, ask of him!
'To furnish these,' replies his wit: ask thine—
Who see the heaven above, the earth below,
Creation everywhere,—these, each and all
Claim certain recognition from the tree
For special service rendered branch and bole,
Top-tuft and tap-root:—for thyself, thus seen,
Palms furnish dates to eat, and leaves to shade,
—Maybe, thatch huts with,—have another use
Than strikes the aphis. So with me, my Son!
I know my own appointed patch i' the world,
What pleasures me or pains there; all outside—
How he, she, it, and even thou, Son, live,
Are pleased or pained, is past conjecture, once
I pry beneath the semblance,—all that 's fit,
To practise with,—reach where the fact may lie
Fathom-deep lower. There 's the first and last
Of my philosophy. Blacks blur thy white?
Not mine! The aphis feeds, nor finds his leaf
Untenable, because a lance-thrust, nay,
Lightning strikes sere a moss-patch close beside,
Where certain other aphids live and love.
Restriction to his single inch of white,
That's law for him, the aphis: but for me,
The man, the larger-souled, beside my stretch
Of blacks and whites, I see a world of woe
All round about me: one such burst of black

Intolerable o'er the life I count
White in the main, and, yea—white's faintest trace
Were clean abolished once and evermore.
Thus fare my fellows, swallowed up in gloom
So far as I discern: how far is that?
God's care be God's! 'T is mine—to boast no joy
Unsobered by such sorrows of my kind
As sully with their shade my life that shines."

"Reflected possibilities of pain,
Forsooth, just chasten pleasure! Pain itself,—
Fact and not fancy, does not this affect
The general color?"

"Here and there a touch
Taught me, betimes, the artifice of things—
That all about, external to myself,
Was meant to be suspected,—not revealed
Demonstrably a cheat,—but half seen through,
Lest white should rule unchecked along the line
Therefore white may not triumph. All the same,
Of absolute and irretrievable
And all-subduing black,—black's soul of black
Beyond white's power to disintensify,—
Of that I saw no sample: such may wreck
My life and ruin my philosophy
To-morrow, doubtless: hence the constant shade
Cast on life's shine,—the tremor that intrudes
When firmest seems my faith in white. Dost ask
'Who is Ferishtah, hitherto exempt
From black experience? Why, if God be just,
Were sundry fellow-mortals singled out
To undergo experience for his sake,
Just that the gift of pain, bestowed on them,
In him might temper to the due degree
Joy's else-excessive largess?' Why, indeed!
Back are we brought thus to the starting-point—
Man's impotency, God's omnipotence,
These stop my answer. Aphis that I am,
How leave my inch-allotment, pass at will
Into my fellow's liberty of range,
Enter into his sense of black and white,
As either, seen by me from outside, seems
Predominatingly the color? Life,
Lived by my fellow, shall I pass into
And myself live there? No—no more than pass
From Persia, where in sun since birth I bask
Daily, to some ungracious land afar,

Told of by travellers, where the night of snow
Smothers up day, and fluids lose themselves
Frozen to marble. How I bear the sun,
Beat though he may unduly, that I know:
How blood once curdled ever creeps again,
Baffles conjecture: yet since people live
Somehow, resist a clime would conquer me,
Somehow provided for their sake must dawn
Compensative resource. 'No sun, no grapes,—
Then, no subsistence!'—were it wisely said?
Or this well-reasoned—'Do I dare feel warmth
And please my palate here with Persia's vine,
Though, over-mounts,—to trust the traveller,—
Snow, feather-thick, is falling while I feast?
What if the cruel winter force his way
Here also?' Son, the wise reply were this:
When cold from over-mounts spikes through and through
Blood, bone and marrow of Ferishtah,—then,
Time to look out for shelter—time, at least,
To wring the hands and cry 'No shelter serves!'
Shelter, of some sort, no experienced chill
Warrants that I despair to find."

"No less,
Doctors have differed here; thou say'st thy say;
Another man's experience masters thine,
Flat controverted by the sourly-Sage,
The Indian witness who, with faculty
Fine as Ferishtah's, found no white at all
Chequer the world's predominating black,
No good oust evil from supremacy,
So that Life's best was that it led to death.
How of his testimony?"

"Son, suppose
My camel told me: 'Threescore days and ten
I traversed hill and dale, yet never found
Food to stop hunger, drink to stay my drouth;
Yet, here I stand alive, which take in proof
That to survive was found impossible!'
'Nay, rather take thou, non-surviving beast,'
(Reply were prompt,) 'on flank this thwack of staff
Nowise affecting flesh that 's dead and dry!
Thou wincest? Take correction twice, amend
Next time thy nomenclature! Call white—white!'
The sourly-Sage, for whom life's best was death,
Lived out his seventy years, looked hale, laughed loud.
Liked—above all—his dinner,—lied, in short."

"Lied is a rough phrase: say he fell from truth
In climbing towards it!—sure less faulty so
Than had he sat him down and stayed content
With thy safe orthodoxy, 'White, all white,
White everywhere for certain I should see
Did I but understand how white is black,
As clearer sense than mine would.' Clearer sense,—
Whose may that be? Mere human eyes I boast,
And such distinguish colors in the main,
However any tongue, that 's human too,
Please to report the matter. Dost thou blame
A soul that strives but to see plain, speak true,
Truth at all hazards? Oh, this false for real,
This emptiness which feigns solidity,—
Ever some gray that 's white and dun that 's black,—
When shall we rest upon the thing itself
Not on its semblance?—Soul—too weak, forsooth,
To cope with fact—wants fiction everywhere!
Mine tires of falsehood: truth at any cost!"

"Take one and try conclusions—this, suppose!
God is all-good, all-wise, all-powerful: truth?
Take it and rest there. What is man? Not God:
None of these absolutes therefore,—yet himself,
A creature with a creature's qualities.
Make them agree, these two conceptions! Each
Abolishes the other. Is man weak,
Foolish and bad? He must be Ahriman,
Co-equal with an Ormuzd, Bad with Good,
Or else a thing made at the Prime Sole Will,
Doing a maker's pleasure—with results
Which—call, the wide world over, 'what must be'—
But, from man's point of view, and only point
Possible to his powers, call—evidence
Of goodness, wisdom, strength? we mock ourselves
In all that 's best of us,—man 's blind but sure
Craving for these in very deed not word,
Reality and not illusions. Well,—
Since these nowhere exist—nor there where cause
Must have effect, nor here where craving means
Craving unfollowed by fit consequence
And full supply, aye sought for, never found—
These—what are they but man's own rule of right?
A scheme of goodness recognized by man,
Although by man unrealizable,—
Not God's with whom to will were to perform:
Nowise performed here, therefore never willed.

What follows but that God, who could the best,
Has willed the worst,—while man, with power to match
Will with performance, were deservedly
Hailed the supreme—provided ... here 's the touch
That breaks the bubble ... this concept of man's
Were man's own work, his birth of heart and brain,
His native grace, no alien gift at all.
The bubble breaks here. Will of man create?
No more than this my hand which strewed the beans
Produced them also from its finger-tips.
Back goes creation to its source, source prime
And ultimate, the single and the sole."

"How reconcile discordancy,—unite
Notion and notion—God that only can
Yet does not,—man that would indeed
But just as surely cannot,—both in one?
What help occurs to thy intelligence?"

"Ah, the beans,—or,—example better yet,—
A carpet-web I saw once leave the loom
And lie at gorgeous length in Ispahan!
The weaver plied his work with lengths of silk
Dyed each to match some jewel as it might,
And wove them, this by that. 'How comes it, friend,'—
(Quoth I)—'that while, apart, this fiery hue,
That watery dimness, either shocks the eye,
So blinding bright, or else offends again,
By dulness,—yet the two, set each by each,
Somehow produce a color born of both,
A medium profitable to the sight?'
'Such medium is the end whereat I aim,'—
Answered my craftsman: 'there 's no single tinct
Would satisfy the eye's desire to taste
The secret of the diamond: join extremes
Results a serviceable medium-ghost,
The diamond's simulation. Even so
I needs must blend the quality of man
With quality of God, and so assist
Mere human sight to understand my Life,
What is, what should be,—understand thereby
Wherefore I hate the first and love the last,—
Understand why things so present themselves
To me, placed here to prove I understand.
Thus, from beginning runs the chain to end,
And binds me plain enough. By consequence,
I bade thee tolerate,—not kick and cuff
The man who held that natures did in fact

Blend so, since so thyself must have them blend
In fancy, if it take a flight so far."

"A power, confessed past knowledge, nay, past thought,
—Thus thought thus known!"

"To know of, think about—
Is all man's sum of faculty effects
When exercised on earth's least atom, Son!
What was, what is, what may such atom be?
No answer! Still, what seems it to man's sense?
An atom with some certain properties
Known about, thought of as occasion needs,
—Man's—but occasions of the universe?
Unthinkable, unknowable to man.
Yet, since to think and know fire through and through
Exceeds man, is the warmth of fire unknown,
Its uses—are they so unthinkable?
Pass from such obvious power to powers unseen,
Undreamed of save in their sure consequence:
Take that, we spoke of late, which draws to ground
The staff my hand lets fall: it draws, at least—
Thus much man thinks and knows, if nothing more."

"Ay, but man puts no mind into such power!
He neither thanks it, when an apple drops,
Nor prays it spare his pate while underneath.
Does he thank Summer though it plumped the rind?
Why thank the other force—whate'er its name—
Which gave him teeth to bite and tongue to taste
And throat to let the pulp pass? Force and force,
No end of forces! Have they mind like man?"

"Suppose thou visit our lord Shalim-Shah,
Bringing thy tribute as appointed. 'Here
Come I to pay my due!' Whereat one slave
Obsequious spreads a carpet for thy foot,
His fellow offers sweetmeats, while a third
Prepares a pipe: what thanks or praise have they?
Such as befit prompt service. Gratitude
Goes past them to the Shah whose gracious nod
Set all the sweet civility at work;
But for his ordinance, I much suspect,
My scholar had been left to cool his heels
Uncarpeted, or warm them—likelier still—
With bastinado for intrusion. Slaves
Needs must obey their master: 'force and force,
No end of forces,' act as bids some force

Supreme o'er all and each: where find that one?
How recognize him? Simply as thou didst
The Shah—by reasoning 'Since I feel a debt,
Behooves me pay the same to one aware
I have my duty, he his privilege.'
Didst thou expect the slave who charged thy pipe
Would serve as well to take thy tribute-bag
And save thee further trouble?"

"Be it so!
The sense within me that I owe a debt
Assures me—somewhere must be somebody
Ready to take his due. All comes to this—
Where due is, there acceptance follows: find
Him who accepts the due! and why look far?
Behold thy kindred compass thee about!
Ere thou wast born and after thou shalt die,
Heroic man stands forth as Shahan-Shah.
Rustem and Gew, Gudarz and all the rest,
How come they short of lordship that 's to seek?
Dead worthies! but men live undoubtedly
Gifted as Sindokht, sage Sulayman's match,
Valiant like Kawah: ay, and while earth lasts
Such heroes shall abound there—all for thee
Who profitest by all the present, past,
And future operation of thy race.
Why, then, o'erburdened with a debt of thanks,
Look wistful for some hand from out the clouds
To take it, when, all round, a multitude
Would ease thee in a trice?"

"Such tendered thanks
Would tumble back to who craved riddance, Son!
—Who but my sorry self? See! stars are out—
Stars which, unconscious of thy gaze beneath,
Go glorifying, and glorify thee too
—Those Seven Thrones, Zurah's beauty, weird Parwin!
Whether shall love and praise to stars be paid
Or—say—some Mubid who, for good to thee
Blind at thy birth, by magic all his own
Opened thine eyes, and gave the sightless sight,
Let the stars' glory enter? Say his charm
Worked while thyself lay sleeping: as he went
Thou wakedst: 'What a novel sense have I!
Whom shall I love and praise?' 'The stars, each orb
Thou standest rapt beneath,' proposes one:
'Do not they live their life, and please themselves,
And so please thee? What more is requisite?'

Make thou this answer: 'If indeed no mage
Opened my eyes and worked a miracle,
Then let the stars thank me who apprehend
That such an one is white, such other blue!
But for my apprehension both were blank.
Cannot I close my eyes and bid my brain
Make whites and blues, conceive without stars' help,
New qualities of color? were my sight
Lost or misleading, would yon red—I judge
A ruby's benefaction—stand for aught
But green from vulgar glass? Myself appraise
Lustre and lustre: should I overlook
Fomalhaut and declare some fen-fire king,
Who shall correct me, lend me eyes he trusts
No more than I trust mine? My mage for me!
I never saw him: if he never was,
I am the arbitrator!' No, my Son!
Let us sink down to thy similitude:
I eat my apple, relish what is ripe—
The sunny side, admire its rarity
Since half the tribe is wrinkled, and the rest
Hide commonly a maggot in the core,—
And down Zerdusht goes with due smack of lips:
But—thank an apple? He who made my mouth
To masticate, my palate to approve,
My maw to further the concoction—Him
I thank,—but for whose work, the orchard's wealth
Might prove so many gall-nuts—stocks or stones
For aught that I should think, or know, or care."

"Why from the world," Ferishtah smiled, "should thanks
Go to this work of mine? If worthy praise,
Praised let it be and welcome: as verse ranks,
So rate my verse: if good therein outweighs
Aught faulty judged, judge justly! Justice says;
Be just to fact, or blaming or approving:
But—generous? No, nor loving!

"Loving! what claim to love has work of mine?
Concede my life were emptied of its gains
To furnish forth and fill work's strict confine,
Who works so for the world's sake—he complains
With cause when hate, not love, rewards his pains.
I looked beyond the world for truth and beauty:
Sought, found, and did my duty."

EPILOGUE

Oh, Love—no, Love! All the noise below, Love,
Groanings all and moanings—none of Life I lose!
All of Life's a cry just of weariness and woe, Love—
"Hear at least, thou happy one!" How can I, Love, but choose?

Only, when I do hear, sudden circle round me
—Much as when the moon's might frees a space from cloud—
Iridescent splendors: gloom—would else confound me—
Barriered off and banished far—bright-edged the blackest shroud!

Thronging through the cloud-rift, whose are they, the faces
Faint revealed yet sure divined, the famous ones of old?
"What"—they smile—"our names, our deeds so soon erases
Time upon his tablet where Life's glory lies enrolled?

"Was it for mere fool's-play, make-believe and mumming,
So we battled it like men, not boylike sulked or whined?
Each of us heard clang God's 'Come!' and each was coming:
Soldiers all, to forward-face, not sneaks to lag behind!

"How of the field's fortune? That concerned our Leader!
Led, we struck our stroke nor cared for doings left and right:
Each as on his sole head, failer or succeeder,
Lay the blame or lit the praise: no care for cowards: fight!"

Then the cloud-rift broadens, spanning earth that 's under,
Wide our world displays its worth, man's strife and strife's success;
All the good and beauty, wonder crowning wonder,
Till my heart and soul applaud perfection, nothing less.

Only, at heart's utmost joy and triumph, terror
Sudden turns the blood to ice: a chill wind disencharms
All the late enchantment! What if all be error—
If the halo irised round my head were, Love, thine arms?

Palazzo Giustinian-Recanati, VENICE:
December 1, 1883.

RAWDON BROWN

"Tutti ga i so gusti, e mi go i mii."
(Venetian saying.)

Mr. Rawdon Brown was an Englishman who went to Venice on some temporary errand, and lived there for forty years, dying in that city in the summer of 1883. He had an enthusiastic love for Venice, and is mentioned in books of travel as one who knew the city thoroughly. The Venetian saying means that "everybody follows his taste as I follow mine." Toni was the gondolier and attendant of Brown. The inscription on Brown's tomb is given in the third and fourth lines. G. W. COOKE.

Sighed Rawdon Brown: "Yes, I 'm departing, Toni!
I needs must, just this once before I die,
Revisit England: Anglus Brown am I,
Although my heart 's Venetian. Yes, old crony—
Venice and London—London 's 'Death the bony'
Compared with Life—that 's Venice! What a sky,
A sea, this morning! One last look! Good-by,
Cà Pesaro! No, lion—I 'm a coney
To weep! I 'm dazzled; 't is that sun I view
Rippling the ... the ... Cospetto, Toni! Down
With carpet-bag, and off with valise-straps!
Bella Venezia, non ti lascio più!"
Nor did Brown ever leave her: well, perhaps
Browning, next week, may find himself quite Brown!

November 28, 1883.

THE FOUNDER OF THE FEAST

Inscribed in an Album presented to Mr. Arthur Chappell, of the Saint James Hall Saturday and Monday popular concerts.

"Enter my palace," if a prince should say—
"Feast with the Painters! See, in bounteous row,
They range from Titian up to Angelo!"
Could we be silent at the rich survey?
A host so kindly, in as great a way
Invites to banquet, substitutes for show
Sound that 's diviner still, and bids us know
Bach like Beethoven; are we thankless, pray?

Thanks, then, to Arthur Chappell,—thanks to him
Whose every guest henceforth not idly vaunts
"Sense has received the utmost Nature grants,
My cup was filled with rapture to the brim,
When, night by night,—ah, memory, how it haunts!—
Music was poured by perfect ministrants,
By Halle, Schumann, Piatti, Joachim.

April 5, 1884.

THE NAMES

At Dr. F. J. Furnivall's suggestion, Browning was asked to contribute a sonnet to the Shakesperean Show-Book of the "Shakesperean Show" held in Albert Hall, London, on May 29-31, 1884, to pay off the debt on the Hospital for Women, in Fulham Road. The poet sent to the committee a sonnet on the names of Jehovah and Shakespeare.

Shakespeare!—to such name's sounding, what succeeds
Fitly as silence? Falter forth the spell,—
Act follows word, the speaker knows full well,
Nor tampers with its magic more than needs.
Two names there are: That which the Hebrew reads
With his soul only: if from lips it fell,
Echo, back thundered by earth, heaven and hell,
Would own "Thou didst create us!" Naught impedes
We voice the other name, man's most of might,
Awesomely, lovingly: let awe and love
Mutely await their working, leave to sight
All of the issue as—below—above—
Shakespeare's creation rises: one remove,
Though dread—this finite from that infinite.

March 12, 1884.

EPITAPH

ON LEVI LINCOLN THAXTER

Born in Watertown, Massachusetts, February 1, 1824.
Died May 31, 1884.

Mr. Thaxter was early a student of Browning's genius and in his later years gave readings from his poems, which were singularly interpretative. The boulder over his grave bears these lines.

Thou, whom these eyes saw never! Say friends true
Who say my soul, helped onward by my song,
Though all unwittingly, has helped thee too?
I gave of but the little that I knew:
How were the gift requited, while along
Life's path I pace, couldst thou make weakness strong!
Help me with knowledge—for Life's Old—Death's New!

R. B. to L. L. T., April, 1885.

Contributed to a volume edited by Andrew Reid, in which a number of leaders of English thought answered the question, "Why I am a Liberal?"

"Why?" Because all I haply can and do,
All that I am now, all I hope to be,—
Whence comes it save from fortune setting free
Body and soul the purpose to pursue,
God traced for both? If fetters, not a few,
Of prejudice, convention, fall from me,
These shall I bid men—each in his degree
Also God-guided—bear, and gayly, too?

But little do or can the best of us:
That little is achieved through Liberty.
Who, then, dares hold, emancipated thus,
His fellow shall continue bound? Not I,
Who live, love, labor freely, nor discuss
A brother's right to freedom. That is "Why."

Robert Browning – A Short Biography

He is the equal of any Victorian Poet that could be mentioned. However, Browning continues to be in the shadow of Tennyson, Arnold, Hopkins, Morris and many others.

Robert Browning was born on May 7th, 1812 in Walworth in the parish of Camberwell, London. He was baptized on June 14th, 1812, at Lock's Fields Independent Chapel, York Street, Walworth.

Browning's early years were certainly very interesting. His mother was an excellent pianist and a very devout evangelical Christian. His father, who worked as a clerk at the Bank of England, was also an artist, scholar, antiquarian, and collector of books and pictures. Indeed, he amassed more than 6,000 volumes of rare books including works in Greek, Hebrew, Latin, French, Italian, and Spanish. For the young and curious Browning, it was a wonderful resource, added to which his father was a guiding force in his education.

Many accounts attest that Browning was already proficient at reading and writing by the age of five. He is said to have been a bright but anxious student and to have studied and learnt Latin, Greek, and French by the time he was fourteen. From fourteen to sixteen he was educated at home, tutored in music, drawing, dancing, and horsemanship. Certainly, language and the arts were two areas the young Browning both absorbed and pushed himself towards.

At the age of twelve he wrote a volume of Byronic verse he called Incondita, which his parents attempted to have published. The attempts were unsuccessful and, disappointed, Browning destroyed the work.

In 1825, a cousin gave Browning a collection of Percy Bysshe Shelley's poetry; Browning was so enamored with the poems that he asked for the rest of Shelley's works for his thirteenth birthday. In fact, Browning then went the extra mile, declaring himself to be both a vegetarian and an atheist in honour of his hero.

Intriguingly it seems that the rejection of his first volume didn't dim his appreciation of other poets, but it appears to have stopped him writing any poems between the ages of thirteen and twenty.

In 1828, Browning enrolled at the newly-opened University of London. He was uncomfortable with the experience and he soon left, anxious to read and absorb at his own pace.

His education which, overall is notably rambling and lacks a structure that many of his artistic contemporaries enjoyed, i.e. excellent public schooling and then a degree at Oxford or Cambridge, may present many of his critics with ammunition to criticize, but alternatively his hap-hazard education certainly contributed to many of the references that baffled both critics and his audience, but they tellingly show the breath and scale of what he could turn words too. What others would call obscure references were, to Browning, remarkably obvious.

Browning's early career was very promising. His long poem Pauline (of which only a fragment was ever finished and published) brought him to the attention of the Pre-Raphaelite master Dante Gabriel Rossetti and his difficult Paracelsus (published in 1835) was warmly admired by both Dickens and Wordsworth.

In the 1830s he met the actor William Macready and was encouraged to develop and turn his talents to the stage by writing verse drama. But these plays, including Strafford, which ran for five nights in 1837, and those contained within the Bells and Pomegranates series, were, for the most part, unsuccessful.

During this period Browning began to discover that his real talents lay in taking a single character and allowing that character to discover more about himself by revealing further personal aspects of himself in his speeches; the dramatic monologue. The techniques he developed through this—especially the use of diction, rhythm, and symbol—are regarded as his most important contribution to poetry. They would later influence such major poets of the 20th Century as Ezra Pound, T. S. Eliot, and Robert Frost.

By 1840, with the publication of Sordello, the tide turned somewhat. Many thought he was being deliberately obscure, opaque beyond measure and his poetry for the next decade or so was not eagerly acquired or talked about.

As Browning attempted to rehabilitate his career he began a relationship with Elizabeth Barrett in 1845. He had read her poems and, being totally charmed by their quality, was determined to meet her. The poetess was better known than the younger Browning but suffered from a debilitating illness and was also subject to the harsh behaviour of her over-bearing father. Nevertheless, the new couple were soon inseparable.

Her father, as he did with any of his children that married, disinherited her. Despite this she had some money from her own resources and sensing that the best outcome for both the relationship and her own health was to move abroad the couple did just that. After a private marriage at St Marylebone Parish Church, in September 1846, they journeyed to Europe to honeymoon in Paris.

Their new life now took them to Italy, first to Pisa and a little later to Florence. There they absorbed life and one another.

But in the short term the literary assault on Browning's work did not let up. He was now criticized by such patrician writers as Charles Kingsley for his abandonment of England for foreign lands. Browning could do little to answer these attacks except to compose with his pen and continue with his poetical journey.

The Browning's were well respected, and even famous. Elizabeth health began to improve, she grew stronger and in 1849, at the age of 43, between four miscarriages, she gave birth to a son, Robert Wiedeman Barrett Browning, whom they nicknamed "Penini" or "Pen",

Intriguingly despite his growing reputation and return to form as a poet he was more often than not known as 'Elizabeth Barrett's husband'.

Work flowed from his pen that was to ensure his reputation as one of England's leading poets. When his collection Men and Women was published in 1855 it contained some of his finest lines. It was dedicated to Elizabeth. Life had begun to smile handsome rewards upon the Brownings.

Victorian society was very much taken with all things spiritualist. It was not enough to have command of much of the globe through Empire, they wished to know and explore wherever they could. The spirit world beckoned their interest. Browning dissented from this view believing it was all a hoax and a fraud. Elizabeth, however, was inclined to believe and this caused several disagreements between the couple.

They attended a séance by Daniel Dunglas Home, in July 1855. (Home was a famous and clamored after Scottish physical medium with the reported ability to levitate and speak with the dead). It is said that during this séance a spirit face materialised. Home then claimed it was the face of Browning's son who had died in infancy. Browning seized the 'materialisation' which turned out to be Home's bare foot. Browning had never lost a son in infancy.

After the séance, Browning wrote an angry letter to The Times, in which he said: "the whole display of hands, spirit utterances etc., was a cheat and imposture."

The Browning's time in Italy were immensely rewarding years for both their personal and professional lives. Browning encouraged her to include Sonnets from the Portuguese in her published works, these beautiful poems are undoubtedly one of the highlights of English love poetry.

Elizabeth had become quite politicised during these years. Engrossed in Italian politics (which was continuing to slowly re-unify the country), she issued a small volume of political poems entitled Poems before Congress (1860) most of which were written to express her sympathy with the Italian cause after the earlier outbreak of The Second Italian Independence War in 1859. In England they caused uproar. Conservative magazines such as Blackwood's and the Saturday Review labelled her a fanatic. She dedicated the book to her husband.

But in 1861 tragedy struck.

The couple had spent the winter of 1860–61 in Rome when Elizabeth's health deteriorated again and they returned to Florence in early June. However, these turned out to be her final weeks. Only morphine would now still the pain. She died in Browning's arms on June 29th, 1861. Browning said that she died "smilingly, happily, and with a face like a girl's .... Her last word was .... "Beautiful".

Her burial took place in the nearby Protestant English Cemetery of Florence. The local people were deeply saddened, and shops closed their doors in grief and respect.

Browning and their son were obviously devastated. Unable to bear being in Florence without Elizabeth they soon returned to London to live at 19 Warwick Crescent, Maida Vale.

As he re-integrated himself back into the London literary scene he began to finally receive the proper praise, respect and reputation that his works deserved.

Browning went on to publish Dramatis Personæ (1864), and The Ring and the Book (1868–1869). The latter, based on an "old yellow book" which told of a seventeenth-century Italian murder trial, received wide and generous critical acclaim. Although by now he was in the twilight of a long and prolific career, that had achieved some notable ups and downs, he was respected and indeed renowned for his talents and works.

In 1878, he revisited Italy for the first time since Elizabeth's death. He would return there on several further occasions but never to Florence.

Such was the esteem he was held in that The Browning Society was founded in 1881. Although he had never obtained a degree (something that set him apart from many other Victorian poets) he was now awarded honorary degrees from Oxford University in 1882 and then the University of Edinburgh in 1884.

In 1887, Browning produced the major work of his later years, Parleyings with Certain People of Importance in Their Day. Browning now spoke with his own voice as he engaged in a series of dialogues with long-forgotten figures of literary, artistic, and philosophic history. Unfortunately, both the critics and public were completely baffled by this.

On April 7th, 1889 Browning attended a dinner party at the home of his friend, the artist Rudolf Lehmann. The highlight of which was a recording made on a wax cylinder on an Edison cylinder phonograph. On the recording, which still exists, Browning recites part of How They Brought the Good News from Ghent to Aix, and can even be heard apologising when he forgets the words.

The recording was first played in 1890 on the anniversary of his death, at a gathering of his admirers, it was said to be the first time anyone's voice 'had been heard from beyond the grave'.

His last work Asolando: Fancies and Facts (1889), returned to his brief and concise lyric verse that was so popular. It was published on the day of his death on December 12th, 1889, Robert Browning was at his son's home Ca' Rezzonico in Venice.

He was buried in Poets' Corner in Westminster Abbey; his grave lies immediately adjacent to that of Alfred Tennyson.

Among the many who have publicly acknowledged their literary debt to him are Henry James, Oscar Wilde, George Bernard Shaw, G. K. Chesterton, Ezra Pound, Jorge Luis Borges, and Vladimir Nabokov.

Robert Browning - A Concise Bibliography

Here follows a list of the plays and poetry volumes published during his lifetime. Poems of particular worth are noted from within those volumes.

Pauline: A Fragment of a Confession (1833)
Paracelsus (1835)
Strafford (play) (1837)
Sordello (1840)
Bells and Pomegranates No. I: Pippa Passes (play) (1841)
    The Year's at the Spring
Bells and Pomegranates No. II: King Victor and King Charles (play) (1842)
Bells and Pomegranates No. III: Dramatic Lyrics (1842)
    Porphyria's Lover
    Soliloquy of the Spanish Cloister
    My Last Duchess
    The Pied Piper of Hamelin
    Count Gismond
    Johannes Agricola in Meditation
Bells and Pomegranates No. IV: The Return of the Druses (play) (1843)
Bells and Pomegranates No. V: A Blot in the 'Scutcheon (play) (1843)
Bells and Pomegranates No. VI: Colombe's Birthday (play) (1844)
Bells and Pomegranates No. VII: Dramatic Romances and Lyrics (1845)
    The Laboratory
    How They Brought the Good News from Ghent to Aix
    The Bishop Orders His Tomb at Saint Praxed's Church
    The Lost Leader
    Home Thoughts from Abroad
    Meeting at Night
Bells and Pomegranates No. VIII: Luria and A Soul's Tragedy (plays) (1846)
Christmas-Eve and Easter-Day (1850)
An Essay on Percy Bysshe Shelley (essay) (1852)
Two Poems (1854)
Men and Women (1855)
    Love Among the Ruins
    A Toccata of Galuppi's
    Childe Roland to the Dark Tower Came
    Fra Lippo Lippi
    Andrea Del Sarto
    The Patriot

www.ingramcontent.com/pod-product-compliance
Lightning Source LLC
Chambersburg PA
CBHW070110070426
42448CB00038B/2484